STANDARDS *for* PROFESSIONAL LEARNING

STANDARDS
for PROFESSIONAL
LEARNING

MetLife Foundation

MetLife Foundation supported the revision and publication of *Standards for Professional Learning*.

Project director: Joellen Killion
Editor: Tracy Crow
Copy editor: Sue Chevalier
Designer: Kitty Black

Reference citation for this book:
Learning Forward. (2011). *Standards for Professional Learning.* Oxford, OH: Author.

Printed in the United States of America
Item #B512
ISBN: 978-1-936630-02-8

Learning Forward
504 S. Locust St.
Oxford, OH 45056
513-523-6029
800-727-7288
Fax: 513-523-0638
Email: office@learningforward.org
www.learningforward.org

About MetLife Foundation

MetLife Foundation is committed to building a secure future for individuals and communities worldwide through a focus on empowering older adults, preparing young people, and building livable communities. In education, MetLife Foundation seeks to strengthen public schools through effective teaching and collaborative leadership, and to prepare students for access to and success in higher education, particularly during the crucial first year. The foundation's grant making is informed by findings from the annual *MetLife Survey of the American Teacher*. More information is available at www.metlife.org.

Contents

Foreword

The primary purpose of professional learning is to improve educator practice and student results. Continuous improvement of individuals, schools, and school systems depends on high-quality professional learning. Professional learning is the primary vehicle available to schools and school systems to strengthen the performance of the education workforce, and the success of educators' daily work depends on it.

For professional learning to deliver on this promise, its conception and design must be based on research and successful practice, and professional learning must be consistently implemented and supported. The newly revised Standards for Professional Learning, the third version of these standards since 1995, define the essential elements of and conditions for professional learning if improvements in educator effectiveness and student learning are to be realized.

Standards for Professional Learning enumerate the conditions, processes, and content of professional learning to support continuous improvement in leadership, teaching, and student learning. The standards stress that effective professional learning is embedded in a culture committed to continuous improvement and informed by data and research on student and educator performance. The standards emphasize that continuous learning and development are essential for the entire education workforce, community members, and government officials who share responsibility for improving student learning. Further, the standards define requisites of effective professional learning so that every educator can demand and advocate for it as a fundamental driver for education reform.

This revision of the Standards for Professional Learning, as with past versions, represents the collective work of multiple education associations, organizations, and agencies. Learning Forward urges the contributors and others to use the standards to affect policy and practice. The standards promote a shared understanding of effective professional learning and offer guidance to various education agencies about how to contribute to ensuring standards-based professional learning for educators.

Learning Forward calls on policy-making authorities at all levels of government to adopt the standards. Decision makers demonstrate their commitment to ensuring effective professional learning by taking this step and, more importantly, holding education systems accountable for meeting the standards. Formal adoption of the standards increases the public's confidence that investments in professional learning come with expectations for high quality and results and that all educators experience the same high level of learning that increases their effectiveness and student learning. Educators, too, can hold their schools and school systems responsible for ensuring that all professional learning meets the standards.

While adopting or endorsing the standards makes a powerful statement about expectations for the quality and results of professional learning, alone it does not guarantee that all professional learning meets the standards. Effective professional learning requires commitment to the principles undergirding the standards as well as a system of accountability that includes monitoring and measuring implementation and results. All educators, community members, and government officials must remain vigilant so that professional learning transforms educator practice and increases student results.

At Learning Forward, we recognize that collaborative engagement strengthens our work. I am deeply grateful to MetLife Foundation for its support for the revision and publication of the third edition of the standards. I am particularly appreciative of the members of the Standards Revision Task Force and the Standards Advisory Team and their facilitator, Joellen Killion, for their commitment to the collective work that resulted in these standards. I acknowledge the many individuals and organizations that provided input on the draft revision because their input strengthened the final product. And I thank in advance the countless educators who will apply the standards in their quest to ensure great teaching for every child every day.

— *Stephanie Hirsh*
Executive Director, Learning Forward

Acknowledgments

The standards revision initiative was made possible with support from MetLife Foundation. Learning Forward is deeply grateful for MetLife Foundation's commitment to effective professional learning for all educators to increase student learning.

Learning Forward is indebted to the following individuals and education associations and organizations for their contribution to the Standards for Professional Learning. Their collective work provides a common language for and shared understanding of effective professional learning that increases educator effectiveness and student learning. This thoughtful group of individuals contributed time, expertise, and perspective so that the standards reflect a broad spectrum of the education community.

STANDARDS REVISION TASK FORCE

American Association of Colleges for Teacher Education ....**Patricia Welch**

American Association of School Administrators...**Ellen Schoetzau**

American Association of School Personnel Administrators...**Doug Gephart**

American Federation of Teachers ....**Alice Gill**

American School Counselor Association...**Jill Cook**

ASCD..**Gayle Owens**

ASCD...**Judy Zimny**

Association of Teacher Educators ....**David Ritchey**

Council of Chief State School Officers...**Kathleen Paliokas**

Learning Forward..**Frederick Brown**

Ingrid Carney

Stephanie Hirsh

Shirley Hord

Jacqueline Kennedy

Joellen Killion

Hayes Mizell

NASSP..**Patti Kinney**

National Association of Elementary School Principals ....**Carol Riley**

National Association of State Boards of Education ....**Bradley Hull**

National Board for Professional Teaching Standards...**Joyce Loveless**

National Conference of State Legislatures ....**Michelle Exstrom**

National Education Association ....**Linda Davin**

National Governors Association...**Tabitha Grossman**

National Middle School Association...**Sue Swaim**

National School Boards Association ....**Lucy Gettman**

Parent Teacher Association..**Audra Akins**

Phi Delta Kappa ....**Joan Richardson**

U.S. Department of Education..**Elizabeth Eisner**

STANDARDS ADVISORY TEAM

American Institutes for Research .... **Claudette Rasmussen**

Asia Society .... **Brandon Wiley**

Australian Professional Teachers Association .... **Susan Gazis**

Center for Teaching Quality .... **Barnett Berry**

Edmonton Regional Learning Consortium .... **Val Olekshy**

Florida Department of Education .... **Eileen McDaniel**

International Reading Association .... **Sakil Malik**

International Society for Technology in Education .... **Lynn Nolan**

Learning Forward British Columbia .... **Audrey Hobbs-Johnson**

London Centre for Leadership in Learning, Institute of Education, University of London .... **Louise Stoll**

Member-at-large .... **Cheryl Green**

Michigan Department of Education .... **Deborah Clemmons**

National Alliance of Black School Educators .... **Lloyd Sain**

National Commission on Teaching and America's Future .... **Tom Carroll**

National Science Teachers Association .... **Christine Anne Royce**

Rose and Smith Associates .... **Raymond Rose**

Teachers of English to Speakers of Other Languages Inc. .... **Judith O'Loughlin**

University of Central Florida .... **Mary Little**

University of Minnesota .... **Lisa Jones**

University of Nevada, Las Vegas .... **Gene Hall**

University of Pennsylvania .... **Laura Desimone**

The Teacher Quality division at the National Education Association provided a home for the Standards Revision Task Force meetings. A special thanks is extended to Linda Davin and her assistants, who made sure to meet the task force's needs.

An initiative of this scope requires the support of many people who are behind the scenes, yet vital to its success. Stephanie Hirsh's visionary leadership of Learning Forward allows the association to thrive as the voice for professional learning. Her commitment to the mission and goals of this organization influences the professional learning experiences of educators across North America and beyond. Hayes Mizell, Learning Forward senior distinguished fellow, and Shirley Hord, Learning Forward scholar laureate, served as members of the task force and also contributed to the introduction of this manual. Their deep knowledge about professional learning and passion for educator learning as a means to increase student learning added richness to the entire revision process. Annette Morales, strategic initiatives manager, skillfully managed hundreds of tasks associated with communication and meeting arrangements. Her attention to detail is remarkable. The Learning Forward publications team, led by

Tracy Crow, director of publications, and including Kitty Black and Sue Chevalier, contributed to the development of this manual. The design and usability of the manual are the responsibility of this team. Jacqueline Kennedy, Learning Forward's associate director of strategic initiatives, worked closely with research assistant Joyce Pollard to assist with the foundational research supporting each standard. Numerous individuals from around the world, including teachers, principals, central office staff members, consultants, university and college faculty, Learning Forward affiliate members and leaders, senior consultants, members of the State Education Agency Professional Development Directors Network, and staff and members of contributing associations and organizations have added their voices to the Standards for Professional Learning by participating in focus groups and providing input on the draft standards. To each of these contributors, who are mostly anonymous, we are extremely grateful. Their interest and comments strengthened the final revision.

I extend my deepest appreciation to each of these contributors.

— Joellen Killion
Deputy Executive Director, Learning Forward

Introduction

Calls for reform spiral around schools, and these calls know no borders. Globally, the public, the press, and the profession share concerns about the effectiveness of education systems. All stakeholders declare their intentions to provide high-quality learning opportunities for all students, no matter what their native language, socioeconomic status, family heritage, traditions, culture, government, or religion. Fortunately, a sophisticated understanding of what this challenge entails is evolving from research and study of successful education systems. However, the knowledge gained is inequitably applied in schools around the globe.

Today's educators are held accountable for preparing all students to meet increasingly rigorous curriculum outcomes and academic standards to be ready for careers and college. Educators and school systems are responsible for ensuring that all students perform at high levels, including those students without access to the experience and resources that support optimal learning.

The public expects educators to be successful with all students throughout their school years, regardless of the profound demographic, economic, cultural, and technological changes that impact student learning. And at the same time, educators, schools, and school systems must meet these challenges in school contexts that are inconsistent and inequitable within and across nations, making it increasingly difficult for all citizens operating in a global environment to have access to an equitable education.

The Standards for Professional Learning do not prescribe how education leaders and public officials address all the challenges related to improving the performance of schools, educators, and students. Instead, the standards focus on one critical aspect of the education system — **professional learning,** sometimes referred to as professional development, staff development, inservice, or training.

A NEW KIND OF EDUCATOR LEARNING

These standards call for a new form of educator learning. The decision to call these Standards for Professional Learning rather than Standards for Professional Development signals the importance of educators taking an active role in their continuous improvement and places emphasis on the learning. By making learning the focus, those who are responsible for professional learning will concentrate their efforts on assuring that learning for educators leads to learning for students. For too long, practices associated with professional development have treated educators as individual, passive recipients of information, and school systems have expected little or no change in practice.

Such development opportunities have often been episodic and unconnected to a shared, systemwide purpose. This form of professional development has consumed tremendous resources over the last decade and produced inadequate results for both educators and students.

The quality of professional learning that occurs when these standards are fully implemented enrolls educators as active partners in determining the focus of their learning, how their learning occurs, and how they evaluate its effectiveness. These educators are part of a team, a school, and a school system that conceive, implement, and evaluate carefully aligned professional learning that responds to individual, team, schoolwide, and systemwide goals for student achievement. The standards give educators the information they need to take leadership roles as advocates for and facilitators of effective professional learning and the conditions required for its success.

Placing the emphasis on professional learning reminds public officials, community members, and educators that educators' continuous improvement affects student learning. Increasing the effectiveness of professional learning is the leverage point with the greatest potential for strengthening and refining the day-to-day performance of educators. For most educators working in schools, professional learning is the singular most accessible means they have to develop the new knowledge, skills, and practices necessary to better meet students' learning needs. If educators are not engaged throughout their careers in new learning experiences that enable them to better serve their students, both educators and students suffer. And if those educators are not learning collaboratively in the context of a systemwide plan for coherent learning tied to a set of goals aligned from classroom to school to school system, their professional learning is less likely to produce its intended results.

In the United States as well as in many other countries, every public school pre-K-12 educator participates in some form of professional learning each year. Professional learning is a component of the extant infrastructure of education systems. Therefore, unlike many proposals for improving public education, there is no need to invent something new or introduce another element into education. It is necessary, however, to improve professional learning's effect on educators and students. Essential to improving professional learning's impact is recognizing and leveraging it systemwide, rather than using professional learning solely as a strategy for individual growth.

This publication is the new iteration of the standards. Like its predecessors, it represents the consensus views of major education associations and agencies representing and serving teachers, school system and school administrators, and education leaders at all levels.

The standards make explicit that the purpose of professional learning is for educators to develop the knowledge, skills, practices, and dispositions they need to help students perform at higher levels. This process of new learning for educators is more complex than most people realize. Indeed, researchers have found that it can take 50 or more hours of sustained professional learning to realize results for students. Students' learning results are paramount. Therefore, educators must make serious efforts to develop and implement practices that effectively produce those results. To support these efforts, professional learning must also be a much more serious enterprise than has sometimes been the case in order to demonstrably benefit educators and their students.

THE ROLE OF THE STANDARDS

It is important for educators to understand what the standards are and are not. They are the essential elements of professional learning that function **in synergy** to enable educators to increase their effectiveness and student learning. All elements are essential to realize the full potential of educator professional learning. The Standards for Professional Learning describe the attributes of effective professional learning to guide the decisions and practices of all persons with the responsibility to fund, regulate, manage, conceive, organize, implement, and evaluate professional learning. It is this latter group that should closely study the standards and systematically use them as a template for organizing professional learning. However, the standards are also a consumers guide for all educators, describing what they should expect and demand of their professional learning, as well as their responsibilities as participants.

The standards are not, however, a workbook, tool kit, or technical assistance guide. They neither address every issue related to professional learning nor provide a road map for creating professional learning that is faithful to the standards. That is intentional. Using the standards to shape more effective professional learning will require study, thought, discussion, and planning. While Learning Forward will produce a suite of print and electronic resources to assist with such efforts, educators and others who want to increase the effect of professional learning should begin by reading the standards deeply. That reading for understanding will most productively occur in a collaborative team where a small group of colleagues reflect on the implications of the standards for their school system or school. From there, team members can begin to imagine and plan how to reshape the professional learning for which they are responsible.

PREREQUISITES FOR PROFESSIONAL LEARNING

Implicit in the standards are several prerequisites for effective professional learning. They are so fundamental that the standards do not identify or describe them. These prerequisites reside where professional learning intersects with professional ethics:

- **Educators' commitment to students, *all* students, is the foundation of effective professional learning.** Committed educators understand that they must engage in continuous improvement to know enough and be skilled enough to meet the learning needs of all students. As professionals, they seek to deepen their knowledge and expand their portfolio of skills and practices, always striving to increase each student's performance. If adults responsible for student learning do not continuously seek new learning, it is not only their knowledge, skills, and practices that erode over time. They also become less able to adapt to change, less self-confident, and less able to make a positive difference in the lives of their colleagues and students. This is why it is important for all educators to engage in professional learning, no matter how proficient they may be at a given point in their careers, and no matter the relative abilities of their students.

- **Each educator involved in professional learning comes to the experience ready to learn.** Professional learning is a partnership among professionals who engage with one another to access or construct knowledge, skills, practices, and dispositions; however, it cannot be effective if educators resist learning. Educators want and deserve high-quality professional learning that is relevant and useful. They are more likely to fully engage in learning with receptive hearts and minds when their school systems, schools, and colleagues align professional learning with the standards.

- **Because there are disparate experience levels and use of practice among educators, professional learning can foster collaborative inquiry and learning that enhances individual and collective per-formance.** This cannot happen unless educators listen to one another, respect one another's experiences and perspectives, hold their students' best interests at the forefront, trust that their colleagues share a common vision and goals, and are honest about their abilities, practices, challenges, and results. Professional accountability for individual and peer results strengthens the profession and results for students.

- **Like all learners, educators learn in different ways and at different rates.** Because some educators have different learning needs than others, professional learning must engage each educator in timely, high-quality learning that meets his or her particular learning needs. Some may benefit from more time than others, different types of learning experiences, or more support as they seek to translate new learning into more productive practices. For some educators, this requires courage to acknowledge their learning needs, and determination and patience to continue learning until the practices are effective and comfortable.

Professional learning is not the answer to all the challenges educators face, but it can significantly increase their capacities to succeed. When school systems, schools, and education leaders organize professional learning aligned with the standards, and when educators engage in professional learning to increase their effectiveness, student learning will increase.

THE LINK TO STUDENT RESULTS

Learning Forward asserts that, when professional learning incorporates the indicators of effectiveness defined in its standards, educator effectiveness and student learning increase. Numerous research studies over the last 20 years confirm that there is a strong relationship between teacher practice and student learning. Studies, too, conclude that professional learning positively influences educator practice — specifically, teacher practice. Studies of school and district leadership conclude that there is a relationship between leadership practices, teaching effectiveness, and student learning. Some studies conclude that there is a relationship between professional learning and student achievement. Many studies of school improvement and education reform name professional learning as one of the top five components of reform efforts. The body of research about effective schools identifies collaboration and professional learning as two characteristics that consistently appear in schools that substantially increase student learning. Some studies of the effects of professional learning have also produced insignificant results on teacher practice or student achievement when measured over a brief period of time, most often at the end of one year of professional learning. Not all professional learning used as a treatment, intervention, or as part of a reform initiative, however, incorporates all the essential elements included in the Standards for Professional Learning. A few studies explore the relationship of policies at various levels of government or system level to the effectiveness of professional learning and its effects.

The field of professional learning will continue to benefit from additional research and evaluation studies that examine the interaction between the effectiveness of the professional learning and its effects on educator practice and student learning. Research in professional learning is sufficient enough to recognize that it is an important lever to improve schools, educator practice, and student learning. With additional research focused on the kind of professional learning that meets the standards specified in the 2011 edition of Standards for Professional Learning, the research may lead more directly to the conclusion that effective professional learning that meets the essential elements described within these standards will produce greater effects for educators and students.

STANDARDS MOVEMENT

Professional learning is a relatively young field. As is true in other fields, professional learning has matured with experience and research. It was not until 1994 that the National Staff Development Council (now Learning Forward) mobilized 10 education organizations to develop Standards for Staff Development. The organization expanded and repeated that process in 2001 with representatives from 19 associations, condensing the standards from three school levels into one unified set, and published a revised version of the Standards for Staff Development. More than 35 state and provincial education agencies and many school systems have either adopted the standards, adapted them, or consulted them as the touchstone for effective professional learning.

RELATIONSHIP BETWEEN PROFESSIONAL LEARNING AND STUDENT RESULTS

1. When professional learning is standards-based, it has greater potential to change what educators know, are able to do, and believe.
2. When educators' knowledge, skills, and dispositions change, they have a broader repertoire of effective strategies to use to adapt their practices to meet performance expectations and student learning needs.
3. When educator practice improves, students have a greater likelihood of achieving results.
4. When student results improve, the cycle repeats for continuous improvement.

This cycle works two ways: If educators are not achieving the results they want, they determine what changes in practice are needed and then what knowledge, skills, and dispositions are needed to make the desired changes. They then consider how to apply the standards so that they can engage in the learning needed to strengthen their practice.

When it began nearly three decades ago, the standards movement in education had as its core purpose to increase the effectiveness and equity of education for all students regardless of their circumstance or postal code. As a long-standing effort to assure that all students achieve at high levels, the standards movement has raised awareness of existing inequities in schools and accountability for results. Whether in the form of national curricula that define equitable expectations for all students or increased expectations for school systems, schools, and educators, efforts to define and implement standards for education continue to be a strong policy lever so that all students achieve at high levels.

The first edition of professional learning standards joined standards in other aspects of education, such as those for specific roles and content-specific curriculum, to establish a set of expectations to assure equity and effectiveness in educator performance. Learning Forward's foundational belief is that reaching high levels of student learning requires corresponding high levels of educator learning. Yet, as occurs with student learning, opportunity, quality, and effectiveness of professional learning have been subject to inequities based on school or school system conditions. If all students are to achieve at high levels, those responsible for their education must have equitable and effective professional learning inextricably tied to student outcomes.

This edition of the standards, drawn from research and based on evidence-based practice, describes a set of expectations for effective professional learning to ensure equity and excellence in educator learning. The standards serve as indicators that guide the learning, facilitation, implementation, and evaluation of professional learning.

Three points underscore the 2011 revision of the standards.

1. There is continuing examination and evaluation of the veracity and practicality of the standards, with feedback solicited from and offered by field practitioners, policy makers, and researchers. The standards are never finished, and Learning Forward's quest for efficiency and effectiveness never ends.

2. To have the greatest influence on professional learning, Learning Forward regularly updates the standards to reflect insights from current research and field experience about professional learning, its application, and its effect on desired outcomes. Learning Forward carefully studies findings to understand needed changes in the standards. To ignore these findings would leave professional learning hopelessly outdated.

3. Standards for professional learning are employed to assure that the quality of learning experiences are not assessed on satisfaction or "happiness coefficient" measures. Instead, the standards and their descriptions establish quality measures related to how well professional learning informs and develops educator knowledge, skills, practices, and dispositions to increase learning for all students.

The seven new standards focus attention on educator learning that relates to successful student learning. The standards require professional learning that is interactive, relevant, sustained, and embedded in everyday practice. They require professional learning that contributes to educators' expertise and the quality of their professional practice, regardless of their role in the education workforce. In this way, equity of access to high-quality education for every student is possible, not just for those lucky enough to attend schools in more advantaged communities.

A HISTORICAL PERSPECTIVE

A grant in 1994 from the Edna McConnell Clark Foundation led to the development of the first set of nationally accepted standards for staff development for middle grades. For some time, leaders of the National Staff Development Council (NSDC), now Learning Forward, discussed the role standards might play in advancing high-quality professional learning in schools. When Hayes Mizell, then the foundation's director of the program for student achievement, issued the invitation to apply for the initial grant, the staff accepted with caveats. The development of the standards would require collaboration among representatives from a significant number of professional associations. The association's leaders wanted educators to have a single, common set of standards for professional learning and urged the contributing associations to join with NSDC to speak with one voice about the elements of effective professional learning. The field benefited from the collective thinking and a consensus mandate for improvement, thanks to the engagement of the associations.

By 2000, changes in the field demanded a review of the standards. The Edna McConnell Clark Foundation again supported the process. The original as well as new associations and individuals contributed to the process. The number of standards was reduced to 12 appropriate at K-12 levels. Once again, the standards were grounded in evidence and research to support the relationship between each standard and changes in educator practice and student learning.

Over time, the standards became the foundation for designing, supporting, and evaluating professional learning. Over the last 15 years, numerous states, organizations, and school systems have adopted policies and studied guidance documents related to the standards. They took these actions with expectations that they would lead to improvements in the quality of professional learning and its results. And, indeed, where the standards were consistently implemented and regularly monitored and evaluated, the standards delivered on their promise.

FAST-FORWARD TO 2011

Since 2001, considerable research has emerged in the field of professional learning, with mixed results. As a result of the research, the field gained clarity about what distinguishes effective from ineffective professional learning. During this decade-long period, there was an explosion of new technologies to support educator learning. In response to these developments, Learning Forward proposed a revision to the standards. With a grant from MetLife Foundation, Learning Forward undertook a revision of the standards for professional learning. New educational reforms, research, and heightened accountability mean that educators and their students are required to meet increasingly rigorous standards. Professional learning that prepares the education workforce to meet these higher standards must also be held to higher standards.

As the first step in developing new standards, Learning Forward undertook a comprehensive examination of the state of professional learning. A team of researchers from Stanford University's Stanford Center for Opportunity Policy in Education led by Linda Darling-Hammond (www. learningforward.org/stateproflearning.cfm) conducted a three-part study that served as the foundation for the standards revision. The study included a review of the literature, a comparison of professional learning practices in the United States and in countries whose students outperform the U.S., an analysis of recent and past practice in professional learning in the U.S., and a case study of state policy related to professional learning. This series of studies was made possible by generous grants from the Bill & Melinda Gates Foundation, The Wallace Foundation, and MetLife Foundation.

The standards development process continued when Learning Forward again invited individuals representing leading education associations to review research and best practice literature to compose standards for their own constituencies, including teachers, principals, superintendents, and school board members. The organizations agreed that a common set of standards to guide the field remained key. They viewed standards as essential for all aspects of professional learning, including planning, implementation, and evaluation at individual, school, and school system levels and as benchmarks for determining future directions for improvement. Rather than developing multiple sets of standards, nations, organizations, states, provinces, and school systems can use the Standards for Professional Learning as a foundation and devote their attention to implementing high-quality professional learning and thereby realize the results of their efforts more quickly.

Learning Forward integrated additional input and contributions into the standards development process by convening focus groups of practitioners, noted authorities, and government officials and circulating the draft standards for public comment.

ORGANIZATION OF THE STANDARDS

The 2011 edition of the Standards for Professional Learning includes several key changes from earlier editions.

Fewer standards: Seven standards emerged from the study of research literature about professional learning. While these seven were included in earlier editions of the standards, they are now more clearly defined, and some aspects are more prominent.

Holistic view: The standards work in partnership with one another. Focusing on some rather than all standards may contribute to the failure of professional learning to deliver on its promised results. These seven standards are not optional for professional learning that intends to increase educator effectiveness and results for all students. The context, process, content organizer is not as prominent in the new standards, yet remains a foundation for the seven standards. For it to be effective, professional learning occurs most often in learning communities; is supported with strong leadership and appropriate resources; is drawn from and measured by data on students, educators, and systems; applies appropriate designs for learning; has substantive implementation support; and focuses on student and educator standards.

Combined content standard: The three previously defined content standards — Equity, Qual-

ity Teaching, and Family Involvement — have been replaced with a single Outcomes standard that incorporates two dimensions, student learning outcomes and educator performance expectations. There are essentially two reasons. First, the Standards for Professional Learning as a whole are focused on increasing results for all students and educators. All seven standards, rather than a single one, focus attention on equity and all drive toward that goal. Second, the educator performance expectations as defined by policy makers include substantially expanded expectations for equity, family and community engagement, and role-specific performance expectations. This combined standard strengthens alignment between educator professional learning and its role in student learning.

Revised stem: The standards begin with a common statement: "Professional learning that increases educator effectiveness and results for all students ... ." This statement confirms the link between educator practice and results for students. The link between educator learning and learning for every student is the purpose of professional learning, and the stem makes that link evident. The statement also emphasizes equity of results. The use of "all" is intentional to elevate the significance of ensuring the success of every student, regardless of race, ethnicity, gender, exceptionality, language, socioeconomic condition, culture, or sexual orientation.

Three areas of focus: The Standards for Professional Learning describe the context, processes, and content for effective professional learning. Learning Communities, Leadership, and Resources standards define the essential conditions for effective professional learning. Without these in place, even the most thoughtfully planned and implemented professional learning may fail. Data, Learning Designs, and Implementation standards describe the attributes of educator learning processes that define quality and effectiveness of professional learning. The single content standard, Outcomes, identifies the essential content of professional learning.

CORE CONCEPTS

Four core concepts are embedded in the stem — educator, effectiveness, results, and all students.

- **Educator** describes the members of the education workforce, those employed within schools and school systems and in other education agencies to provide direct or indirect services to students. Educators include both the professional and support staff who contribute to student learning.

- **Effectiveness** refers to educators' capacity to meet performance expectations, implement evidence-based practices, create and sustain conditions for effective learning, and increase student learning. Effectiveness is evident in performance as defined by role expectations and professional standards and by the results of an educator's work.

- **Results** refers to all aspects of student growth and development. Academic success is the primary results area, and it is coupled with social and emotional learning in the overall development of students. Academic, social, and emotional development work together to ensure student success. Student learning is assessed through multiple measures, both formative and summative, that provide evidence that students are succeeding in meeting the expected curriculum outcomes and development indicators. These measures include, and are not limited to, daily classroom assessments such as student work samples and performances; educator and parent observations; student self-assessments; periodic common or benchmark assessments, portfolios of work, projects or performances; and standardized assessments.

- *All* **students** signifies that educators' professional responsibility and professional learning are driven by the belief that education for all students, not just some, is fundamental to the well-being of a global society. Without equitable opportunities and universal high expectations for all students, societal, political, and economic infrastructures suffer.

FULFILLING THE PROMISE

Continuous learning provides members of any profession with new understandings, insights, and ideas for how to develop essential skills and behaviors. In short, it enables the profession's members to refine and extend their knowledge, skills, practices, and dispositions related to their specific role and context. Individuals are unlikely to seek the services of an automobile mechanic, plumber, or surgeon who isn't up-to-date on the latest field knowledge, studies, products, and procedures. Students deserve nothing less from the educators who serve them.

As educators invest in continuous improvement through professional learning, they demonstrate professionalism and commitment to students. School systems that invest in professional learning and build coherence throughout the system demonstrate commitment to human capital development and acknowledge that investment in educator learning is a significant lever in improving student achievement.

The use of Standards for Professional Learning by school systems and educators supports a high level of quality of the professional learning. Further, use of the standards to plan, facilitate, and evaluate professional learning promises to heighten the quality of educator learning, performance of all educators, and student learning. Increased educator effectiveness makes possible a shift from current reality to the preferred outcomes of enhanced student learning results — a goal to which all educators subscribe.

— *Hayes Mizell,* Distinguished Senior Fellow
— *Shirley Hord,* Scholar Laureate
— *Joellen Killion,* Deputy Executive Director
— *Stephanie Hirsh,* Executive Director
Learning Forward

The standards work in partnership with one another.

STANDARDS
for PROFESSIONAL LEARNING

Professional learning that increases educator effectiveness and results for all students ...

Standards for Professional Learning

LEARNING COMMUNITIES: Professional learning that increases educator effectiveness and results for all students occurs within learning communities committed to continuous improvement, collective responsibility, and goal alignment.

LEADERSHIP: Professional learning that increases educator effectiveness and results for all students requires skillful leaders who develop capacity, advocate, and create support systems for professional learning.

RESOURCES: Professional learning that increases educator effectiveness and results for all students requires prioritizing, monitoring, and coordinating resources for educator learning.

DATA: Professional learning that increases educator effectiveness and results for all students uses a variety of sources and types of student, educator, and system data to plan, assess, and evaluate professional learning.

LEARNING DESIGNS: Professional learning that increases educator effectiveness and results for all students integrates theories, research, and models of human learning to achieve its intended outcomes.

IMPLEMENTATION: Professional learning that increases educator effectiveness and results for all students applies research on change and sustains support for implementation of professional learning for long-term change.

OUTCOMES: Professional learning that increases educator effectiveness and results for all students aligns its outcomes with educator performance and student curriculum standards.

Professional learning that increases educator effectiveness and results for all students **occurs within learning communities committed to continuous improvement, collective responsibility, and goal alignment.**

LEARNING COMMUNITIES

LEADERSHIP

RESOURCES

DATA

Professional learning within communities requires continuous improvement, promotes collective responsibility, and supports alignment of individual, team, school, and school system goals. Learning communities convene regularly and frequently during the workday to engage in collaborative professional learning to strengthen their practice and increase student results. Learning community members are accountable to one another to achieve the shared goals of the school and school system and work in transparent, authentic settings that support their improvement.

ENGAGE IN CONTINUOUS IMPROVEMENT

Learning communities apply a cycle of continuous improvement to engage in inquiry, action research, data analysis, planning, implementation, reflection, and evaluation. Characteristics of each application of the cycle of continuous improvement are:

- The use of data to determine student and educator learning needs;
- Identification of shared goals for student and educator learning;
- Professional learning to extend educators' knowledge of content, content-specific pedagogy, how students learn, and management of classroom environments;
- Selection and implementation of appropriate evidence-based strategies to achieve student and educator learning goals;
- Application of the learning with local support at the work site;
- Use of evidence to monitor and refine implementation; and
- Evaluation of results.

DEVELOP COLLECTIVE RESPONSIBILITY

Learning communities share collective responsibility for the learning of all students within the school or school system. Collective responsibility brings together the entire education community, including members of the education workforce — teachers, support staff, school system staff, and administrators — as well as families, policy makers, and other stakeholders, to increase effective teaching in every classroom. Within learning communities, peer accountability rather than formal or administrative accountability ignites commitment to professional learning. Every student benefits from the strengths and expertise of every educator when communities of educators learn together and are supported by local communities whose members value education for all students.

Collective participation advances the goals of a whole school or team as well as those of individuals. Communities of caring, analytic, reflective, and inquiring educators collaborate to learn what is necessary to increase student learning. Within learning communities, members exchange feedback about their practice with one another, visit each other's classrooms or work settings, and share resources. Learning community members strive to refine their collaboration, communication, and relationship skills to work within and across both internal and external systems to support student learning. They develop norms of collaboration and relational trust and employ processes and structures that unleash expertise and strengthen capacity to analyze, plan,

implement, support, and evaluate their practice.

While some professional learning occurs individually, particularly to address individual development goals, the more one educator's learning is shared and supported by others, the more quickly the culture of continuous improvement, collective responsibility, and high expectations for students

and educators grows. Collective responsibility and participation foster peer-to-peer support for learning and maintain a consistent focus on shared goals within and across communities. Technology facilitates and expands community interaction, learning, resource archiving and sharing, and knowledge construction and sharing. Some educators may meet with peers virtually in local or global communities to focus on individual, team, school, or school system improvement goals. Often supported through technology, cross-community communication within schools, across schools, and among school systems reinforces shared goals, promotes knowledge construction and sharing, strengthens coherence, taps educators' expertise, and increases access to and use of resources.

Communities of learners may be various sizes, include members with similar or different roles or responsibilities, and meet frequently face-to-face, virtually, or through a combination. Educators may be members of multiple learning communities. Some communities may include members who share common students, areas of responsibility, roles, interests, or goals. Learning communities tap internal and external expertise and resources to strengthen practice and student learning. Because the education system reaches out to include students, their families, community members, the education workforce, and public officials who share responsibility for student achievement, some learning communities may include representatives of these groups.

CREATE ALIGNMENT AND ACCOUNTABILITY

Professional learning that occurs within learning communities provides an ongoing system of support for continuous improvement and implementation of school and systemwide initiatives. To avoid fragmentation among learning communities and to strengthen their contribution to school and system goals, public officials and school system leaders create policies that establish formal accountability for results along with the support needed to achieve results. To be effective, these policies and supports align with an explicit vision and goals for successful learning communities. Learning communities align their goals with those of the school and school system, engage in continuous professional learning, and hold all members collectively accountable for results.

The professional learning that occurs within

learning communities both supports and is supported by policy and governance, curriculum and instruction, human resources, and other functions within a school system. Learning communities bridge the knowing-doing gap by transforming macro-level learning — knowledge and skill development — into micro-level learning — the practices and refinements necessary for full implementation in the classroom or workplace. When professional learning occurs within a system driven by high expectations, shared goals, professionalism, and peer accountability, the outcome is deep change for individuals and systems.

RELATED RESEARCH

Bolam, R., McMahon, A., Stoll, L., Thomas, S., & Wallace, M. (with Greenwood, A., et al.). (2005, May). *Creating and sustaining effective professional learning communities* (Research Brief RB637). Nottingham, United Kingdom: Department for Education and Skills.

Hord, S.M. (Ed.). (2004). *Learning together, leading together: Changing schools through professional learning communities.* New York: Teachers College Press & NSDC.

Lieberman, A. & Miller, L. (Eds.) (2008). *Teachers in professional communities: Improving teaching and learning.* New York: Teachers College Press.

McLaughlin, M.W. & Talbert, J.E. (2001). *Professional communities and the work of high school teaching.* Chicago: University of Chicago Press.

Saunders, W.M., Goldenberg, C.N., & Gallimore, R. (2009, December). Increasing achievement by focusing grade-level teams on improving classroom learning: A prospective, quasi-experimental study of Title I schools. *American Educational Research Journal, 46*(4), 1006-1033.

NOTES

Professional learning that increases educator effectiveness and results for all students **requires skillful leaders who develop capacity, advocate, and create support systems for professional learning.**

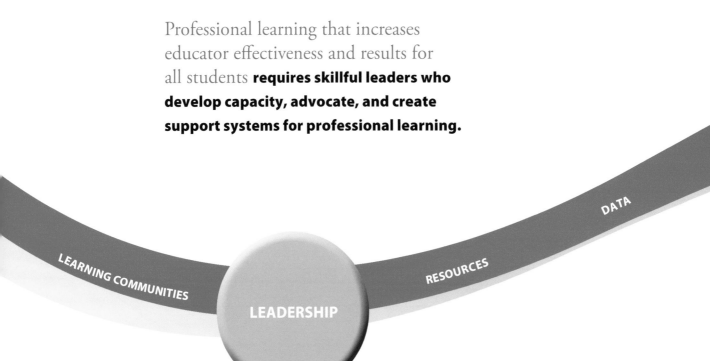

LEARNING COMMUNITIES

LEADERSHIP

RESOURCES

DATA

L eaders throughout the pre-K-12 education community recognize effective professional learning as a key strategy for supporting significant school and school system improvements to increase results for all students. Whether they lead from classrooms, schools, school systems, technical assistance agencies, professional associations, universities, or public agencies, leaders develop their own and others' capacity to learn and lead professional learning, advocate for it, provide support systems, and distribute leadership and responsibility for its effectiveness and results.

DEVELOP CAPACITY FOR LEARNING AND LEADING

Leaders hold learning among their top priorities for students, staff, and themselves. Leaders recognize that universal high expectations for all students require ambitious improvements in curriculum, instruction, assessment, leadership practices, and support systems. These improvements require effective professional learning to expand educators' knowledge, skills, practices, and dispositions. All leaders demand effective professional learning focused on substantive results for themselves, their colleagues, and their students. Leaders artfully combine deep understanding of and cultural responsiveness to the community they serve with high expectations and support for results to achieve school and school system goals. They embed professional learning into the organization's vision by communicating that it is a core function for improvement and by establishing and maintaining a public and persistent focus on educator professional learning.

Leaders of professional learning are found at the classroom, school, and system levels. They set the agenda for professional learning by aligning it to classroom, school, and school system goals for student and educator learning, using data to monitor and measure its effects on educator and student performance. They may facilitate professional learning, coach and supervise those who facilitate it, or do both. As facilitators of professional learning, they apply a body of technical knowledge and skills to plan, design, implement, and evaluate professional learning. As coaches and supervisors of those who facilitate professional learning, they develop expertise in others about effective professional learning, set high standards for their performance, and use data to give frequent, constructive feedback.

To engage in constructive conversations about the alignment of student and educator performance, leaders cultivate a culture based on the norms of high expectations, shared responsibility, mutual respect, and relational trust. They work collaboratively with others, such as school and system-based resource personnel and external technical assistance providers, so that all educators engage in effective job-embedded or external professional learning to meet individual, team, school, and system goals.

Systems that recognize and advance shared leadership promote leaders from all levels of the organizations. Leaders can hold formal roles, such as principal, instructional coach, or task force chair, for long periods of time or informal roles, such as voluntary mentor or spokesperson, for shorter periods. All leaders share responsibility for student achievement among members of the school and

community. Leaders hold themselves and others accountable for the quality and results of professional learning. Leaders work collaboratively with others to create a vision for academic success and set clear goals for student achievement based on educator and student learning data.

ADVOCATE FOR PROFESSIONAL LEARNING

Leaders clearly articulate the critical link between increased student learning and educator professional learning. As supporters of professional

learning, they apply understanding of organizational and human changes to design needed conditions, resources, and other supports for learning and change.

As advocates for professional learning, leaders make their own career-long learning visible to others. They participate in professional learning within and beyond their own work environment. Leaders consume information in multiple fields to enhance their leadership practice. Through learning, they clarify their values and beliefs and their influence on others and on the achievement of organizational goals. Their actions model attitudes and behavior they expect of all educators.

Leaders engage with all stakeholders — those within the education workforce, students, public officials who oversee schools, parent and community organizations, and the business community — to communicate the importance of professional learning. They engage parents and other caretakers in the education of their children and establish partnerships with key community organizations to promote the success of all students.

CREATE SUPPORT SYSTEMS AND STRUCTURES

Skillful leaders establish organizational systems and structures that support effective professional learning and ongoing continuous improvement. They equitably distribute resources to accomplish individual, team, school, and school system goals. Leaders actively engage with policy makers and decision makers so that resources, policies, annual calendars, daily schedules, and structures support professional learning to increase student achievement. Leaders create and align policies and guidelines to ensure effective professional learning within their school systems or schools. They work within national, regional, and local agencies to adopt standards, monitor implementation, and evaluate professional learning's effectiveness and results.

RELATED RESEARCH

Knapp, M.S., Copland, M.A., & Talbert, J.E. (2003, February). *Leading for learning: Reflective tools for school and district leaders.* Seattle, WA: Center for the Study of Teaching and Policy.

Leithwood, K., Louis, K.S., Anderson, S., & Wahlstrom, K. (2004). *How leadership influences student learning: A review of research for the Learning from Leadership Project.* New York: Wallace Foundation.

Spillane, J.P., Halverson, R., & Diamond, J.B. (2001, April). Investigating school leadership practice: A distributed perspective. *Educational Researcher, 30*(3), 23-27.

Waters, J.T., Marzano, R.J., & McNulty, B.A. (2003). *Balanced leadership: What 30 years of research tells us about the effect of leadership on student achievement.* Aurora, CO: McREL.

York-Barr, J. & Duke, K. (2004, Fall). What do we know about teacher leadership? Findings from two decades of scholarship. *Review of Educational Research, 74*(3), 255-316.

NOTES

_____

_____

_____

_____

_____

_____

_____

_____

_____

_____

_____

_____

_____

_____

_____

_____

_____

_____

Professional learning that increases educator effectiveness and results for all students **requires prioritizing, monitoring, and coordinating resources for educator learning.**

LEARNING COMMUNITIES

LEADERSHIP

RESOURCES

DATA

Effective professional learning requires human, fiscal, material, technology, and time resources to achieve student learning goals. How resources are allocated for professional learning can overcome inequities and achieve results for educators and students. The availability and allocation of resources for professional learning affect its quality and results. Understanding the resources associated with professional learning and actively and accurately tracking them facilitates better decisions about and increased quality and results of professional learning.

PRIORITIZE HUMAN, FISCAL, MATERIAL, TECHNOLOGY, AND TIME RESOURCES

Resources for professional learning include staff, materials, technology, and time, all dependent on available funding. How these resources are priori-

tized to align with identified professional learning needs affects access to, quality of, and effectiveness of educator learning experiences. Decisions about resources for professional learning require a thorough understanding of student and educator learning needs, clear commitment to ensure equity in resource allocation, and thoughtful consideration of priorities to achieve the intended outcomes for students and educators.

Staff costs are a significant portion of the resource investment in professional learning. Costs in this category include school and school system leaders and other specialized staff who facilitate or support school- or school system-based professional learning, such as instructional coaches, facilitators, and mentors, as well as salary costs for educators when professional learning occurs within their workday. The time leaders commit to professional learning, either their own or for those they supervise, is a cost factor because it is time these leaders are investing in professional learning; managing this time is another area of responsibility for leaders.

Time allocated for professional learning is another significant investment. Education systems worldwide have schedules that provide time in the school day for teacher collaboration and planning to increase student learning. Learning time for educators may extend into after-school meetings, summer extended learning experiences, and occasional times during the workday when students are not present.

Professional learning embedded into educators' workdays increases the opportunity for all educators to receive individual, team, or school-based support within the work setting to promote continuous improvement. Dedicated job-embedded learning time elevates the importance of continuous, career-long learning as a professional responsibility of all educators and aligns the focus of their learning to the identified needs of students they serve. Including substantive time for professional learning, 15% or more, within the workday shifts some costs for external professional learning to support job-embedded professional learning.

Technology and material resources for professional learning create opportunities to access information that enriches practice. Use of high-speed broadband, web-based and other technologies, professional journals and books, software, and a comprehensive learning management system is essential to support individual and collaborative professional learning. Access to just-in-time learning resources and participation in local or global communities or networks available to individuals or teams of educators during their workday expand opportunities for job-embedded professional learning.

Investments in professional learning outside the school or workplace supplement and advance job-embedded professional learning. To increase alignment and coherence between job-embedded and external professional learning, both must address

the individual, school, and school system goals for educator and student learning.

When economic challenges emerge, schools and school systems often reduce investments in professional learning. In high-performing countries, professional learning is valued so highly as a key intervention to improve schools that reducing it is not an option. Top-performing businesses frequently increase training and development in challenging times. In lean times, professional learning is especially important to prepare members of the workforce for the changes they will experience, maintain and increase student achievement, develop flexibility to detect and adapt to new economic conditions and opportunities, and sustain employee morale, retention, commitment, and expertise.

MONITOR RESOURCES

Resources for professional learning come from many sources, including government allocations, public and private agencies, and educators themselves. Tracking and monitoring these resources is challenging, yet essential. Some costs, such as those for staff, registrations, consultants, materials, stipends for mentor teachers, and relief teachers, are relatively easy to track. Others, such as the portion of time educators are engaged in job-embedded professional learning and technology used for professional learning, are more difficult to monitor. Yet without a consistent and comprehensive process to track and monitor resources, it is difficult to evaluate the appropriateness or effectiveness of their allocation and use.

The level of funding for professional learning in schools varies tremendously. Some studies on professional learning in public schools have suggested that the investments range from less than 1% of total operating expenses to as high as 12%. In the highest-performing countries, investments in professional learning for educators, particularly teachers and principals, are much higher. Decisions about funding must specifically address inequities in learning needs and opportunities to learn and be given highest priority so that that all students and the educators who serve them have the resources to achieve at the highest levels.

COORDINATE RESOURCES

The coordination of resources for professional learning is essential to their appropriate and effective use. With funding for professional learning, school improvement, and other reform initiatives coming from multiple sources and for multiple pur-poses, ensuring alignment and effectiveness in resource use is paramount to ensuring success. School and school system leaders are primarily responsible for coordinating resources. However, all educators have a shared responsibility to understand and contribute to decisions about and monitor the effectiveness of resources allocated for professional learning.

To make certain that resources invested in professional learning achieve their intended results, school system leaders regularly convene representatives of all stakeholders to examine and recommend changes to policies, regulations, and agreements related to professional learning.

RELATED RESEARCH

Abdal-Haqq, I. (1996). *Making time for teacher professional development.* Washington, DC: ERIC Clearinghouse on Teaching and Teacher Education. (ERIC Document Reproduction Service No. ED 400259)

Chambers, J.G., Lam, I., & Mahitivanichcha, K. (2008, September). *Examining context and challenges in measuring investment in professional development: A case study of six school districts in the Southwest region* (Issues & Answers Report, REL 2008-No. 037). Washington, DC: U.S. Department of Education, Institute of Education Sciences, National Center for Education Evaluation and Regional Assistance, Regional Educational Laboratory Southwest.

Haslam, M.B. (1997, Fall). How to rebuild a local professional development infrastructure. *NAS Getting Better by Design.* Arlington, VA: New American Schools.

Odden, A., Archibald, S., Fermanich, M., & Gallagher, H.A. (2002). A cost framework for professional development. *Journal of Education Finance, 28*(1), 51-74.

OECD. (2011). *Strong performers and successful reformers in education: Lessons from PISA for the United States.* Paris: OECD Publishing.

NOTES

_____

_____

_____

_____

_____

_____

_____

_____

_____

_____

_____

_____

_____

_____

_____

_____

_____

_____

_____

_____

Professional learning that increases educator effectiveness and results for all students **uses a variety of sources and types of student, educator, and system data to plan, assess, and evaluate professional learning.**

LEARNING COMMUNITIES

LEADERSHIP

RESOURCES

DATA

Data from multiple sources enrich decisions about professional learning that leads to increased results for every student. Multiple sources include both quantitative and qualitative data, such as common formative and summative assessments, performance assessments, observations, work samples, performance metrics, portfolios, and self-reports. The use of multiple sources of data offers a balanced and more comprehensive analysis of student, educator, and system performance than any single type or source of data can. However, data alone do little to inform decision making and increase effectiveness.

Thorough analysis and ongoing use are essential for data to inform decisions about professional learning, as is support in the effective analysis and use of data.

ANALYZE STUDENT, EDUCATOR, AND SYSTEM DATA

Data about students, educators, and systems are useful in defining individual, team, school, and system goals for professional learning. Probing questions guide data analysis to understand where students are in relationship to the expected curriculum standards and to identify the focus for educator professional learning. Student data include formal and informal assessments, achievement data such as grades and annual, benchmark, end-of-course, and daily classroom work, and classroom assessments. Other forms of data, such as those that cover demographics, engagement, attendance, student perceptions, behavior and discipline, participation in extracurricular programs, and post-graduation education, are useful in understanding student learning needs, particularly if they are analyzed by student characteristics.

Knowing student learning needs guides decisions about educator professional learning, yet student data alone are insufficient. A comprehensive understanding of educator learning needs is essential to planning meaningful professional learning. Sample data to consider for identifying goals for educator learning include preparation information, performance on various assessments, educator perceptions, classroom or work performance, student results, and individual professional learning goals.

Changes at the student and educator levels are best sustained when school and system-level learning occur simultaneously. School and system administrators also engage in data collection and analysis to determine changes in policy, procedures, fiscal resources, human resources, time, or technology, for example, needed to support school- and team-based learning. Administrators might analyze data about inputs, such as fiscal, personnel, and time allocation; outputs, such as frequency of participation, level of engagement, and type of communication; and outcomes, such as changes in educator practice and student achievement.

ASSESS PROGRESS

Data also are useful to monitor and assess progress against established benchmarks. At the classroom level, teachers use student data to assess the effectiveness of the application of their new learning. When teachers, for example, design assessments and scoring guides and engage in collaborative analysis of student work, they gain crucial

information about the effect of their learning on students. Evidence of ongoing increases in student learning is a powerful motivator for teachers during the inevitable setbacks that accompany complex change efforts.

At the school level, leadership teams use data to monitor implementation of professional learning and its effects on educator practice and student

learning. Engaging teams of teacher leaders and administrators in analyzing and interpreting data, for example, provides them a more holistic view of the complexity of school improvement and fosters collective responsibility and accountability for student results.

Frequent collection and use of data about inputs, outputs, and outcomes of professional learning reinforce the cycle of continuous improvement by allowing for ongoing adjustments in the learning process to increase results for students, educators, and systems. Ongoing data collection, analysis, and use, especially when done in teams, provide stakeholders with information that sustains momentum and informs continuous improvement.

EVALUATE PROFESSIONAL LEARNING

Those responsible for professional learning implement and maintain standards for professional learning and use the standards to monitor, assess, and evaluate it. Well-designed evaluation of professional learning provides information needed to increase its quality and effectiveness. Evaluation of professional learning also provides useful information for those who advocate for professional learning; those responsible for engaging in, planning, facilitating, or supporting professional learning; and those who want to know about the contribution of professional learning to student achievement.

Internal and external evaluators conduct evaluations of professional learning. Some professional learning, such as programs funded through grants or other special funding, requires formal, external evaluations. Whether or not an external evaluation is required, all professional learning should be evaluated on an ongoing basis for its effectiveness and results. For example, a school system might engage in a rigorous evaluation of its mentoring and induction program every three years and collect other output data annually for formative assessment.

Questions that guide the evaluation of professional learning address its worth, merit, and effects. Evaluation questions are designed based on the goals of professional learning and the various audiences interested in the evaluation. For example, federal policy makers might want to know if the investment in professional learning contributed to changes in student achievement. School system leaders may want to know if increasing time for teacher collaboration and adding coaches result in

changes in teacher practice and student learning. Teachers might want to know if the implementation of new instructional practices increased their effectiveness with certain types of students. Evaluators design a process to answer the evaluation questions, gather quantitative and qualitative data from various sources, analyze and interpret the data, form conclusions, and recommend future actions.

Evaluation of professional learning includes examination of data related to inputs, outputs, and outcomes. Evaluation of professional learning follows a rigorous process, international standards for evaluation, and a code of ethics for evaluators.

RELATED RESEARCH

Datnow, A. (1999, April). *How schools choose externally developed reform designs* (Report No. 35). Baltimore: Center for Research on the Education of Students Placed At Risk.

Desimone, L., Porter, A., Garet, M., Yoon, K.S., & Birman, B. (2002, Summer). Effects of professional development on teachers' instruction: Results from a three-year longitudinal study. *Educational Evaluation and Policy Analysis, 24*(2), 81-112.

Griffith, P.L., Kimmel, S.J., & Biscoe, B. (2010, Winter). Teacher professional development for at-risk preschoolers: Closing the achievement gap by closing the instruction gap. *Action in Teacher Education, 31*(4), 41-53.

Reeves, D.B. (2010). *Transforming professional development into student results.* Alexandria, VA: ASCD.

Torgesen, J., Meadows, J.G., & Howard, P. (n.d.). *Using student outcome data to help guide professional development and teacher support: Issues for Reading First and K-12 reading plans.* Tallahassee, FL: Florida Center for Reading Research.

NOTES

Professional learning that increases educator effectiveness and results for all students **integrates theories, research, and models of human learning to achieve its intended outcomes.**

LEARNING COMMUNITIES

LEADERSHIP

RESOURCES

DATA

Integrating theories, research, and models of human learning into the planning and design of professional learning contributes to its effectiveness. Several factors influence decisions about learning designs, including the goals of the learning, characteristics of the learners, their comfort with the learning process and one another, their familiarity with the content, the magnitude of the expected change, educators' work environment, and resources available to support learning. The design of professional learning affects its quality and effectiveness.

APPLY LEARNING THEORIES, RESEARCH, AND MODELS

Cognitive psychologists, neuroscientists, and educators have studied how learning occurs for nearly a century. The resulting theories, research, and models of human learning shape the underly-

ing framework and assumptions educators use to plan and design professional learning. While multiple designs exist, many have common features, such as active engagement, modeling, reflection, metacognition, application, feedback, ongoing support, and formative and summative assessment, that support change in knowledge, skills, dispositions, and practice.

Professional learning occurs in face-to-face, online, and hybrid settings. Some professional learning focuses on individual learning, while other forms focus on team-based or whole-school learning. Most professional learning occurs as a part of the workday, while other forms occur outside the school day. Both formal and informal designs facilitate and organize educator learning. Some learning designs use structured processes such as courses or workshops. Others are more fluid to allow for adjustments in the learning process. Some learning designs require team members or external experts as facilitators, while others are individually organized. Learning designs use synchronous or asynchronous interactions, live or simulated models and experiences, and print and nonprint resources to present information, model skills and procedures, provide low-risk practice, and support transfer to the workplace.

Job-embedded learning designs engage individuals, pairs, or teams of educators in professional learning during the workday. Designs for job-embedded learning include analyzing student data, case studies, peer observation or visitations, simulations, co-teaching with peers or specialists, action research, peer and expert coaching, observing and analyzing demonstrations of practice, problem-based learning, inquiry into practice, student observation, study groups, data analysis, constructing and scoring assessments, examining student or educator work, lesson study, video clubs, professional reading, or book studies. Learners and facilitators of learning may weave together multiple designs within on-site, online, or hybrid learning to achieve identified goals and to differentiate learning designs to meet the unique needs of individual learners. Learning designs that occur during the workday and engage peers in learning facilitate ongoing communication about learning, develop a collaborative culture with peer accountability, foster professionalism, and support transfer of the learning to practice.

Technology is rapidly enhancing and extending opportunities for professional learning. It particularly facilitates access to, sharing, construction,

and analysis of information to enhance practice. Technology exponentially increases possibilities for personalizing, differentiating, and deepening learning, especially for educators who have limited access to on-site professional learning or who are eager to reach beyond the boundaries of their own work setting to join local or global networks to enrich their learning.

SELECT LEARNING DESIGNS

When choosing designs for professional learning, educators consider multiple factors. The first is the intended outcome, drawn from analysis of student and educator learning needs. Learning

designs that engage adult learners in applying the processes they are expected to use facilitate the learning of those behaviors by making them more explicit. Effective designs for professional learning assist educators in moving beyond comprehension of the surface features of a new idea or practice to developing a more complete understanding of its purposes, critical attributes, meaning, and connection to other approaches. To increase student learning, educator learning provides many opportunities for educators to practice new learning with ongoing assessment, feedback, and coaching so the learning becomes fully integrated into routine behaviors.

Educators are responsible for taking an active role in selecting and constructing learning designs that facilitate their own and others' learning. They choose appropriate learning designs to achieve their individual, team, or school goals. Educators' learning characteristics and preferences also inform decisions about learning designs. Learners' backgrounds, experiences, beliefs, motivation, interests, cognitive processes, professional identity, and commitment to school and school system goals affect how educators approach professional learning and the effectiveness of various learning designs. Decisions about learning designs consider all phases of the learning process, from knowledge and skill acquisition to application, reflection, refinement, assessment, and evaluation. Learning designers consider how to build knowledge, develop skills, transform practice, challenge attitudes and beliefs, and inspire action.

PROMOTE ACTIVE ENGAGEMENT

Active engagement in professional learning promotes change in educator practice and student learning. Active engagement occurs when learners interact during the learning process with the content and with one another. Educator collaborative learning consistently produces strong, positive effects on achievement of learning outcomes. Active engagement respects adults as professionals and gives them significant voice and choice in shaping their own learning. Through active engagement, ed-

ucators construct personal meaning of their learning, are more committed to its success, and identify authentic applications for their learning. Active learning processes promote deep understanding of new learning and increase motivation to implement it. Active learning processes include discussion and dialogue, writing, demonstrations, inquiry, reflection, metacognition, co-construction of knowledge, practice with feedback, coaching, modeling, and problem solving. Through exploration of individual and collective experiences, learners actively construct, analyze, evaluate, and synthesize knowledge and practices.

RELATED RESEARCH

Croft, A., Coggshall, J.G., Dolan, M., & Powers, E. (with Killion, J.). (2010, April). *Job-embedded professional development: What it is, who's responsible, and how to get it done well* (Issue Brief). Washington, DC: National Comprehensive Center for Teacher Quality.

Dede, C. (Ed.) (2006). *Online professional development for teachers: Emerging models and methods.* Cambridge, MA: Harvard Education Press.

Garet, M.S., Porter, A., Desimone, L., Birman, B., & Yoon, K.S. (2001, Winter). What makes professional development effective? Results from a national sample of teachers. *American Educational Research Journal, 38*(4), 915-945.

Joyce, B. & Showers, B. (2002). *Student achievement through staff development.* Alexandria, VA: ASCD.

Penuel, W.R., Fishman, B.J., Yamaguchi, R., & Gallagher, L.P. (2007, December). What makes professional development effective? Strategies that foster curriculum implementation. *American Educational Research Journal, 44*(4), 921-958.

NOTES

Professional learning that increases educator effectiveness and results for all students **applies research on change and sustains support for implementation of professional learning for long-term change.**

LEARNING COMMUNITIES

LEADERSHIP

RESOURCES

DATA

The primary goals for professional learning are changes in educator practice and increases in student learning. This is a process that occurs over time and requires support for implementation to embed the new learning into practices. Those responsible for professional learning apply findings from change process research to support long-term change in practice by extending learning over time. They integrate a variety of supports for individuals, teams, and schools. Finally, they integrate constructive feedback and reflection to support continuous improvement in practice that allows educators to move along a continuum from novice to expert through application of their professional learning.

APPLY CHANGE RESEARCH

Effective professional learning integrates research about individual, organization, technical, and adaptive change through supporting and sustaining implementation for long-term change. Those responsible for professional learning, whether leaders, facilitators, or participants, commit to long-term change by setting clear goals and maintaining high expectations for implementation with fidelity. Drawing from multiple bodies of research about change, leaders provide and align resources, including time, staff, materials, and technology, to initiate and sustain implementation. Individuals, peers, coaches, and leaders use tools and metrics to gather evidence to monitor and assess implementation. Leaders and coaches model salient practices and maintain a sustained focus on the goals and strategies for achieving them. Leaders create and maintain a culture of support by encouraging stakeholders to use data to identify implementation challenges and engage them in identifying and recommending ongoing refinements to increase results. They engender community support for implementation by communicating incremental successes, reiterating goals, and honestly discussing the complexities of deep change.

Understanding how individuals and organizations respond to change and how various personal, cognitive, and work environment factors affect those experiencing change gives those leading, facilitating, or participating in professional learning the ability to differentiate support, tap educators' strengths and talents, and increase educator effectiveness and student learning.

SUSTAIN IMPLEMENTATION

Professional learning produces changes in educator practice and student learning when it sustains implementation support over time. Episodic, periodic, or occasional professional learning has little effect on educator practice or student learning because it rarely includes ongoing support or opportunities for extended learning to support implementation. Formal professional learning, such as online, on-site, or hybrid workshops, conferences, or courses, is useful to develop or expand knowledge and skills, share emerging ideas, and network learners with one another. To bridge the knowing-doing gap and integrate new ideas into practice, however, educators need three to five years of ongoing implementation support that includes opportunities to deepen their understanding and address problems associated with practice.

Ongoing support for implementation of professional learning takes many forms and occurs at the implementation site. It may be formalized through ongoing workshops designed to deepen understanding and refine educator practice. It occurs through coaching, reflection, or reviewing results. It may occur individually, in pairs, or in collaborative learning teams when educators plan, implement, analyze, reflect, and evaluate the integration of their professional learning into their practice. It occurs

within learning communities that meet to learn or refine instructional strategies; plan lessons that integrate the new strategies; share experiences about implementing those lessons; analyze student work together to reflect on the results of use of the strategies; and assess their progress toward their defined goals. School- and system-based coaches provide extended learning opportunities, resources for implementation, demonstrations of the practices, and specific, personalized guidance. Peer support groups, study groups, peer observation, co-teaching, and co-planning are other examples of extended support. When educators work to resolve challenges related to integration of professional learning, they support and sustain implementation. Professional learning is a process of continuous improvement focused on achieving clearly defined student and educator learning goals rather than an event defined by a predetermined number of hours.

PROVIDE CONSTRUCTIVE FEEDBACK

Constructive feedback accelerates implementation by providing formative assessment through the learning and implementation process. It provides specific information to assess practice in relationship to established expectations and to adjust practice so that it more closely aligns with those expectations. Feedback from peers, coaches, supervisors, external experts, students, self, and others offers information for educators to use as they refine practices. Reflection is another form of feedback in which a learner engages in providing constructive feedback on his or her own or others' practices.

Effective feedback is based on clearly defined expected behaviors, acknowledges progress toward expectations, and provides guidance for achieving full implementation. Giving and receiving feedback about successes and improvements require skillfulness in clear, nonjudgmental communication based on evidence, commitment to continuous improvement and shared goals, and trusting, respectful relationships between those giving and receiving feedback.

To add validity and reliability to the feedback process, educators develop and use common, clear expectations that define practice so that the feedback is focused, objective, relevant, valid, and purposeful. Educators consider and decide what evidence best demonstrates the expected practices and their results. Frequent feedback supports continuous improvement, whereas occasional feedback is often considered evaluative. Feedback about progress toward expected practices provides encouragement to sustain the desired changes over time. Tools that define expected behaviors facilitate data collection and open, honest feedback.

RELATED RESEARCH

Bandura, A. (1986). *Social foundations of thought and action: A social cognitive theory.* Englewood Cliffs, NJ: Prentice-Hall.

Fullan, M. (2007). *The new meaning of educational change* (4th ed.). New York: Teachers College Press.

Hall, G. & Hord, S. (2011). *Implementing change: Patterns, principles, and potholes* (3rd ed.). Boston: Allyn & Bacon.

Huberman, M. & Miles, M.B. (1984). *Innovation up close: How school improvement works.* New York: Plenum.

Supovitz, J.A. & Turner, H.M. (2000, November). The effects of professional development on science teaching practices and classroom culture. *Journal of Research in Science Teaching, 37*(9), 963-980.

NOTES

Professional learning that increases educator effectiveness and results for all students **aligns its outcomes with educator performance and student curriculum standards.**

LEARNING COMMUNITIES

LEADERSHIP

RESOURCES

DATA

For all students to learn, educators and professional learning must be held to high standards. Professional learning that increases results for all students addresses the learning outcomes and performance expectations education systems designate for students and educators. When the content of professional learning integrates student curriculum and educator performance standards, the link between educator learning and student learning becomes explicit, increasing the likelihood that professional learning contributes to increased student learning. When systems increase the stakes for students by demanding high, equitable outcomes, the stakes for professional learning increase as well.

MEET PERFORMANCE STANDARDS

Educator performance standards typically de-lineate the knowledge, skills, practices, and dispositions of highly effective educators. Standards guide preparation, assessment, licensing, induction, practice, and evaluation. Frequently regulated by government agencies, standards establish requirements for educator preparation, define expectations of an effective workforce, guide career-long professional learning of the education workforce, and set fair and reliable indicators of effectiveness for measuring educator performance.

Teacher standards specify what teachers need to know and do to deliver on the promise of an effective, equitable education for every student. Typical areas included in teacher standards are knowledge, skills, and dispositions related to content knowledge; pedagogy; pedagogical content knowledge; assessment; understanding how students learn; understanding how students' cognitive, social, emotional, and physical development influences their

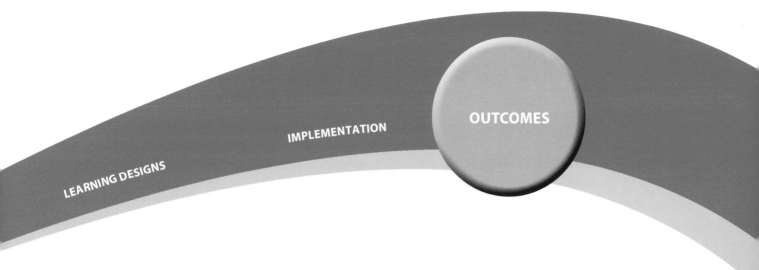

learning; engaging students with diverse cultures, language, gender, socioeconomic conditions, and exceptionalities; engaging families and communities in student learning; creating learning environments; professional growth and development; and professional collaboration.

Standards for school and system leaders, like teacher standards, describe what effective leaders know and do so that every student and educator performs at high levels. Whether for teacher leaders or school or school system administrators, these standards delineate specific expectations for preparation, assessment, licensure, professional learning, practice, and evaluation of those engaged in leadership roles within a school or school system. Typical areas covered in leader standards include establishing a vision and strategic plan for effective learning; leading learning of students and staff; developing workplace culture to support learning; engaging in their own professional learning; managing facilities, workforce, operations, and resources; establishing effective relationships and communication systems; managing change; sharing leadership with others; engaging staff and families in decision making; understanding and responding to the diverse needs of students and communities; understanding and responding to cultural, political, social, legal, and financial contexts; and securing individual, team, school, and whole system accountability for student success.

Standards for other members of the education workforce delineate the unique knowledge,

skills, qualities, and dispositions required of those in specialized roles. These roles include school nurses, guidance counselors, librarians, instructional coaches, resource personnel, classroom assistants, and other instructional and noninstructional staff who are vital to schools and school systems. Standards for advanced or specialized certification guide professional learning for those who seek career advancement or differentiated roles.

ADDRESS LEARNING OUTCOMES

Student learning outcomes define equitable expectations for all students to achieve at high levels and hold educators responsible for imple-

menting appropriate strategies to support student learning. Learning for educators that focuses on student learning outcomes has a positive effect on changing educator practice and increasing student achievement. Whether the learning outcomes are developed locally or nationally and are defined in content standards, courses of study, curriculum, or curricular programs, these learning outcomes serve as the core content for educator professional learning to support effective implementation and results. With student learning outcomes as the focus, professional learning deepens educators' content knowledge, pedagogical content knowledge, and understanding of how students learn the specific discipline. Using student learning outcomes as its outcomes, professional learning can model and engage educators in practices they are expected to implement within their classrooms and workplaces.

BUILD COHERENCE

Coherence requires that professional learning builds on what educators have already learned; focuses on learning outcomes and pedagogy aligned with national or local curriculum and assessments for educator and student learning; aligns with educator performance standards; and supports educators in developing sustained, ongoing professional communication with other educators who are engaged in similar changes in their practice. Any single professional learning activity is more likely to be effective in improving educator performance and student learning if it builds on earlier professional learning and is followed up with later, more advanced work to become a part of a coherent set of opportunities for ongoing professional learning. Coherence also ensures that professional learning is a part of a seamless process that begins in the preparation program and continues throughout an educator's career and aligns tightly with the expectations for effectiveness defined in performance standards and student learning outcomes.

RELATED RESEARCH

Blank, R.K., de las Alas, N., & Smith, C. (2007, February). *Analysis of the quality of professional development programs for mathematics and science teachers: Findings from a cross-state study.* Washington, DC: Council of Chief State School Officers.

Borko, H. (2004, November). Professional development and teacher learning: Mapping the terrain. *Educational Researcher, 33*(8), 3-15.

Cohen, D. & Hill, H. (2000). Instructional policy and classroom performance: The mathematics reform in California. *Teachers College Record, 102*(2), 294-343.

Kennedy, M. (1998, March). Education reform and subject matter knowledge. *Journal of Research in Science Teaching, 35*(3), 249-263.

Shulman, L.S. (2000, January-February). Teacher development: Roles of domain expertise and pedagogical knowledge. *Journal of Applied Developmental Psychology, 21*(1), 129-135.

NOTES

These standards stimulate dialogue, discussion, and analysis that lead to increased effectiveness in professional learning regardless of the state of current practice.

Appendices

How to use
STANDARDS FOR PROFESSIONAL LEARNING

Standards for Professional Learning are designed to set policies and shape practice in professional learning. Improvement is a continuous process without a beginning or end. Because professional learning is at the core of every effort to increase educator effectiveness and results for all students, its quality and effectiveness cannot be left to chance. These standards set clear expectations for professional learning. The standards will guide the efforts of individuals, teams, school and school system staff, public agencies and officials, and nonprofit and for-profit associations or organizations engaged in setting policy, organizing, providing, facilitating, managing, participating in, monitoring, or measuring professional learning to increase educator effectiveness and results for all students.

These standards stimulate dialogue, discussion, and analysis that lead to increased effectiveness in professional learning regardless of the state of current practice. The suggestions here offer ideas about how various types of readers may use this publication to deepen their understanding of effective professional learning and how to strengthen professional learning for all educators.

INDIVIDUALS

Individual educators, those working in schools, education systems, or public or private agencies, can benefit from gaining a deeper understanding of effective professional learning. By studying the standards, individuals will be stronger advocates for effective professional learning for themselves and their colleagues. Specifically, individuals can:

- Study the standards to develop a foundational knowledge about effective professional learning.

- Benchmark existing opportunities for professional learning against the standards to identify strengths and areas for improvement.

- Use the standards to develop proposals to school or system leaders or public officials to improve existing practices in professional learning.

- Apply the standards in the development of recommendations or plans for individual, team, school, or school system professional learning.

- Use the standards to request improvements in professional learning in which they participate.

- Advocate for effective professional learning to increase educator effectiveness and results for all students.

- Apply the standards to the planning, design, facilitation, and evaluation of professional learning they lead.

- Use the standards to develop the essential knowledge, skills, dispositions, and practices for new roles that require facilitating professional learning.

SCHOOL STAFF

School staff, either in teams or as a whole, use the standards to strengthen school-based professional learning, particularly to address team and school improvement goals and increase student learning. Specifically, school staffs can:

- Study the standards to develop a foundational knowledge about effective professional learning.

- Benchmark existing opportunities for professional learning against the standards to identify strengths and areas for improvement.

- Study the standards as a part of the school improvement planning process to make recommendations for improving current practice in professional learning.

- Apply the standards to the planning, design, facilitation, and evaluation of all team- and school-based professional learning.

- Share the standards with external assistance providers who facilitate professional learning with school staff.

- Use the standards as a part of school reviews and accreditation or inspectorate visits to explain how staff members are engaged in continuous learning.

- Use the standards to frame requests to the school system for assistance with professional learning.

- Apply the standards to the work of teacher leaders, coaches, curriculum leaders, grade-level, team, division, or department leaders.

- Share the standards with parents, guardians, and community members to foster their advocacy and support for professional learning as a means to increase student learning.

- Bring the standards into all program implementation or improvement discussions.

SCHOOL SYSTEM STAFF

Most school systems share responsibility for effective professional learning with school leaders. To increase the effectiveness of professional learning, school system leaders can:

- Benchmark existing opportunities for professional learning against the standards to identify strengths and areas for improvement.

- Study the standards as a part of the school system improvement planning process to make recommendations for improving current practice in professional learning.

- Apply the standards to the planning, design, facilitation, and evaluation of all professional learning provided by the school system.

- Share the standards with external assistance providers who facilitate professional learning with school staff.

- Develop a review process to hold schools and external assistance providers accountable for meeting the standards.

- Use the standards for school board or trustee development.

- Apply the standards to the school system's comprehensive plan for professional learning.

- Use the standards to develop the capacity of teacher leaders and principals to be effective leaders and facilitators of professional learning.

- Create a review process to apply to all proposed professional learning to assess whether it aligns with the standards.

- Develop model plans and programs for profes-

sional learning as a resource to develop a deeper understanding of what the standards look like in practice.

- Use the standards as the basis for recognizing and publicizing successful professional learning.

- Use the standards as criteria for evaluating the effectiveness of all professional learning.

- Develop video-based scenarios of standards-based professional learning.

- Post the standards on or link to the standards from the school system's web site.

- Study policies related to professional learning to determine if they align with the standards and make necessary revisions to strengthen alignment.

- Prepare a resolution that the school trustees adopt the standards as expectations for all professional learning.

- Bring the standards into all program implementation or improvement discussions.

- Disseminate the standards to parents, guardians, and community members to develop their understanding about the role of professional learning in student success.

- Develop or make available resources to school and school system staff and school and school system leaders to develop their understanding and implementation of the standards.

- Restrict funding for professional learning to programs that integrate all the standards to increase the likelihood for success.

GOVERNMENT AGENCY STAFF

Those who support school systems and schools either in an elected or appointed capacity have a responsibility to support effective professional learning. They can:

- Study the standards as a part of the school or system improvement planning process to make recommendations for improving current practice in professional learning.

- Use the standards to develop criteria for all agency-supported professional learning.

- Require evaluation of professional learning based on the standards.

- Embed the standards as criteria for school and school system planning documents.

- Use the standards as the basis for reviewing all requests for agency support of professional learning or for awarding credit or continuing education units for professional learning.

- Embed the standards into criteria for review and/or accreditation of schools and school systems.

- Disseminate the standards to community members to build their awareness and support for effective professional learning to increase student learning.

- Embed the standards into policies, regulations, or guidance about professional learning.

- Develop a recognition program for schools or school systems implementing the standards.

- Create demonstration schools or school systems to develop the capacity of other schools and school systems to understand and implement effective professional learning.

- Use the standards to plan, design, facilitate, and evaluate professional learning for agency staff.

- Develop or make available resources to agency staff and school and school system leaders to develop their understanding and implementation of the standards.

- Develop a review process to hold school systems and external assistance providers accountable for meeting the standards.

- Restrict funding for professional learning to programs that integrate all the standards to increase the likelihood for success.

Standards summary

Standards for Professional Learning	Core elements of each standard
LEARNING COMMUNITIES: Professional learning that increases educator effectiveness and results for all students occurs within learning communities committed to continuous improvement, collective responsibility, and goal alignment.	• Engage in continuous improvement. • Develop collective responsibility. • Create alignment and accountability.
LEADERSHIP: Professional learning that increases educator effectiveness and results for all students requires skillful leaders who develop capacity, advocate, and create support systems for professional learning.	• Develop capacity for learning and leading. • Advocate for professional learning. • Create support systems and structures.
RESOURCES: Professional learning that increases educator effectiveness and results for all students requires prioritizing, monitoring, and coordinating resources for educator learning.	• Prioritize human, fiscal, material, technology, and time resources. • Monitor resources. • Coordinate resources.
DATA: Professional learning that increases educator effectiveness and results for all students uses a variety of sources and types of student, educator, and system data to plan, assess, and evaluate professional learning.	• Analyze student, educator, and system data. • Assess progress. • Evaluate professional learning.
LEARNING DESIGNS: Professional learning that increases educator effectiveness and results for all students integrates theories, research, and models of human learning to achieve its intended outcomes.	• Apply learning theories, research, and models. • Select learning designs. • Promote active engagement.
IMPLEMENTATION: Professional learning that increases educator effectiveness and results for all students applies research on change and sustains support for implementation of professional learning for long-term change.	• Apply change research. • Sustain implementation. • Provide constructive feedback.
OUTCOMES: Professional learning that increases educator effectiveness and results for all students aligns its outcomes with educator performance and student curriculum standards.	• Meet performance standards. • Address learning outcomes. • Build coherence.

Crosswalk WITH PREVIOUS STANDARDS

2011 Standards for Professional Learning	2001 Standards for Staff Development
LEARNING COMMUNITIES: Professional learning that increases educator effectiveness and results for all students occurs within learning communities committed to continuous improvement, collective responsibility, and goal alignment.	**LEARNING COMMUNITIES:** Staff development that improves the learning of all students organizes adults into learning communities whose goals are aligned with those of the school and district. **COLLABORATION:** Staff development that improves the learning of all students provides educators with the knowledge and skills to collaborate.
LEADERSHIP: Professional learning that increases educator effectiveness and results for all students requires skillful leaders who develop capacity, advocate, and create support systems for professional learning.	**LEADERSHIP:** Staff development that improves the learning of all students requires skillful school and district leaders who guide continuous instructional improvement.
RESOURCES: Professional learning that increases educator effectiveness and results for all students requires prioritizing, monitoring, and coordinating resources for educator learning.	**RESOURCES:** Staff development that improves the learning of all students requires resources to support adult learning and collaboration.
DATA: Professional learning that increases educator effectiveness and results for all students uses a variety of sources and types of student, educator, and system data to plan, assess, and evaluate professional learning.	**DATA-DRIVEN:** Staff development that improves the learning of all students uses disaggregated student data to determine adult learning priorities, monitor progress, and help sustain continuous improvement. **EVALUATION:** Staff development that improves the learning of all students uses multiple sources of information to guide improvement and demonstrate its impact.

2011 Standards for Professional Learning	2001 Standards for Staff Development
LEARNING DESIGNS: Professional learning that increases educator effectiveness and results for all students integrates theories, research, and models of human learning to achieve its intended outcomes.	**DESIGN:** Staff development that improves the learning of all students uses learning strategies appropriate to the intended goal. **RESEARCH-BASED:** Staff development that improves the learning of all students prepares educators to apply research to decision making.
IMPLEMENTATION: Professional learning that increases educator effectiveness and results for all students applies research on change and sustains support for implementation of professional learning for long-term change.	**LEARNING:** Staff development that improves the learning of all students applies knowledge about human learning and change.
OUTCOMES: Professional learning that increases educator effectiveness and results for all students aligns its outcomes with educator performance and student curriculum standards.	**EQUITY:** Staff development that improves the learning of all students prepares educators to understand and appreciate all students, create safe, orderly, and supportive learning environments, and hold high expectations for their academic achievement. **QUALITY TEACHING:** Staff development that improves the learning of all students deepens educators' content knowledge, provides them with research-based instructional strategies to assist students in meeting rigorous academic standards, and prepares them to use various types of classroom assessments appropriately. **FAMILY INVOLVEMENT:** Staff development that improves the learning of all students provides educators with knowledge and skills to involve families and other stakeholders appropriately.